Ocean Explorer!

Angela Royston

Crabtree Publishing Company

www.crabtreebooks.com

Author: Angela Royston
Editors: Kathy Middleton
Crystal Sikkens
Project coordinator: Kathy Middleton
Production coordinator: Ken Wright
Prepress technicians: Ken Wright
Margaret Amy Salter

Every effort has been made to trace copyright holders and to obtain their permission for use of copyright material. The authors and publishers would be pleased to rectify any error or omission in future editions. All the Internet addresses given in this book were correct at the time of going to press. The author and publishers regret any inconvenience caused if addresses have changed or sites have ceased to exist, but can accept no responsibility for any such changes.

Picture Credits:
Dreamstime: Amandamhanna: page 20; Michael Ansell: page 10; Alain Lacroix: page 21; Ne_fall_foliage: page 11
Photolibrary: Splashdown Direct: page 18; Volvox volvox: page 15
Shutterstock: cover; Subbotina Anna: page 4; Rich Carey: page 5; Steven Gibson: page 7; Idreamphoto: page 6; Knumina: page 8; Levent Konuk: page 12; Joze Maucec: page 16; NatalieJean: page 17; Nautilus Media: page 19; Nataliya Taratunina: page 9; Tonobalaguerf: page 13; Joanna Zopoth-Lipiejko: page 14

Library and Archives Canada Cataloguing in Publication

Royston, Angela
Ocean explorer! / Angela Royston.

(Crabtree connections)
Includes index.
ISBN 978-0-7787-7842-4 (bound).--ISBN 978-0-7787-7864-6 (pbk.)

1. Oceanography--Juvenile literature. 2. Ocean--Juvenile literature. I. Title. II. Series: Crabtree connections

GC21.5.R69 2011   j578.77   C2011-900596-4

Library of Congress Cataloging-in-Publication Data

Royston, Angela, 1945-
Ocean explorer! / Angela Royston.
p. cm. -- (Crabtree connections)
Includes index.
ISBN 978-0-7787-7864-6 (pbk. : alk. paper) --
ISBN 978-0-7787-7842-4 (reinforced library binding : alk. paper)
1. Oceanography--Juvenile literature. 2. Ocean--Juvenile literature.
I. Title.
GC21.5.R686 2011
578.77--dc22
                              2011001328

Crabtree Publishing Company
www.crabtreebooks.com   1-800-387-7650

Printed in Canada/062020/CPC20200608

Published in Canada
Crabtree Publishing
616 Welland Ave.
St. Catharines, Ontario
L2M 5V6

Published in the United States Crabtree Publishing
347 Fifth Ave
Suite 1402-145
New York, NY 10016

Contents

Dive In.. 4

Seabed Swimmer 6

Sandy Star.. 8

Ink Bomb!.. 10

Fantastic Fish...................................... 12

Crab Attack 14

Super Spiky 16

Giant Shark!.. 18

Stinging Sea Jellies 20

Glossary... 22

Further Reading.................................. 23

Index.. 24

Dive In

The ocean is full of amazing creatures. I saw a lot on my **dive**.

Undersea horse

First I saw a sea horse. Its head looks a bit like a horse's head!

Sea horses have long, curly tails.

My dive photos

I used a special camera to take photos. It works underwater.

Giddy up!

Seabed Swimmer

Next I saw a turtle swimming across the **seabed**. It was looking for **shellfish** to eat.

Tough stuff

A turtle has a tough **shell** around its body.

A sea turtle uses its **flippers** to swim.

flipper

shell

In hiding

A sea turtle lays her eggs on the beach. They **hatch** into sea baby turtles.

I'm hungry!

Sandy Star

Then I saw a sea star on the seabed. It had five arms and looked like a star.

Ooops!

The sea star was also looking for shellfish. Sea stars are strong and can open up a shell to eat the animal inside.

I'm hungry!

8

No head

A sea star does not have a head. Its eyes are at the end of its arms.

If a sea star loses an arm, a new one will grow back.

Ink Bomb!

Then I saw something long and wavy in front of me. It was the arm of an octopus.

Ink attack

When I tried to touch the octopus, it squirted me with black **ink**. Then it zoomed away.

arm ————————

Can't catch me!

Suckers

An octopus uses its **suckers** to hold on to rocks and food.

sucker

An octopus has eight arms.

Fantastic Fish

I saw lots of fish swimming below me. They were many different shapes and colors.

Striped swimmers

Many kinds of colorful fish swim around **coral reefs**. I liked the striped ones best.

Some fish have lots of stripes.

Long sword

A swordfish uses its "sword" or sharp beak, to help it catch fish to eat.

Look at me!

Crab Attack

Next I spotted a crab. It crept out from under a stone. I dived down to get a closer look.

Crab grab

The crab had eight legs and two big claws. It grabbed me with one of its claws!

eye

claw

Watch out!

14

Giant crabs

The biggest crab is as big as a car!

leg

The crab's eyes stand out from its head.

Super Spikey

Some sea urchins were clinging to the rocks. Sea urchins look like plants, but they are animals.

Ouch!

Sea urchins are covered with sharp spikes. I was careful not to step on one!

Some sea urchins have **poison** in their spikes.

Shells and spikes

A sea urchin's shell is round and covered in spikes.

Don't step on me!

Giant Shark!

As I swam back to the surface, a basking shark swam by. It is the second-biggest shark in the world.

Big mouth

A basking shark has a huge mouth, but I wasn't afraid. It doesn't attack people.

Open wide

Basking sharks eat tiny animals.

Spotty shark

This spotted fish is a small shark. It is called a dogfish.

Stinging Sea Jellies

As I swam to the beach, I saw a stinging sea jelly. Its body was made of jelly and it had long tentacles.

Deadly sting

The tentacles give a **poisonous** sting. The sting from some sea jellies can kill you!

Wibble wobble

Baby sea jellies

Sea jellies are tiny at first. They float and feed in the sea.

tentacle

This sea jelly is shaped like an umbrella.

Glossary

coral reefs Structures that feel like rock but are made of millions of tiny sea animals

dive Going down beneath the surface of the water

flippers Wide, flat body parts used for swimming.

hatch To break out of an egg

ink Liquid that an octopus squirts to protect itself

poison Something that is harmful if eaten or if it enters the blood of a living thing

seabed Ground at the bottom of the sea

shell Hard cover that protects an animal's body

shellfish Sea creatures that have a shell

suckers Parts that grip on to rocks or other surfaces

tentacle Long feeler that a sea animal uses to move and feel. Some tentacles sting.

Further Reading

Websites

This website tells you about several of the sea animals in this book. Go down to 'Invertebrates' and click on the animals in the list. You can find them at:
http://animals.nationalgeographic.com/animals/facts

Play games and find out more about sea creatures at:
http://learnenglishkids.britishcouncil.org/category/ general-themes/sea-animals

Books

Planet Animal: Under the Sea by Anita Ganeri, Carlton Books (2010).

The ABCs of Oceans by Bobbie Kalman, Crabtree Publishing (2008).

The Living Ocean series, Crabtree Publishing (2003-2006).

Baby Animals in Ocean Habitats by Bobbie Kalman, Crabtree Publishing (2001).

Index

basking sharks 18

camera 5
claws 14
coral reefs 12
crabs 14–15

dogfish 19

eggs 7
eyes 9, 15

fish 12–13
flippers 6

hatch 7

ink 10

octopuses 10–11

poison 16, 20

seabed 6, 8
sea horses 4
sea jellies 20–21
sea stars 8–9
sea turtles 6–7
sea urchins 16–17
sharks 18–19
shell 6
shellfish 6
spikes 16–17
sting 20
suckers 11
swordfish 13

tails 4
tentacles 20